Letters
from a Marine

By: Rick, Bob & Steven

ENVELOPE 2 (envelope 1not found)

From:

PFC A. D. Katz 136-8507

"A" Company, 3rd Tk BN

3RD Marine DIV. FMF

c/o FPO San Francisco, Calif.

Postmarked by US Navy, 4 May 1954

All my last one for the day in a

Addressed to   SHEILAH BIBNICK

1130 FOREST AVE

ST. LOUIS (10) Mo.

May 3, 1954

Dear Sheilah –

It was great to receive your answer to my letter. I really do enjoy to get mail from you. You sound like a real swell girl. After being over here for 10 months it is real nice to get more mail from home than ever before. Especially from a nice girl like you. I don't know if my sister told you about me but sometimes I write silly letters. You see I always write the way I feel. Sometimes it sounds funny to the person at home and even sometimes they get mad. So you see what you are in for? Hope that you are very understanding because that's the people I can really get along with. You told me you were going to write and tell me all about the play you were in at school. Well, don't forget. I just can't wait to hear all about it. I'll bet you'll be the "hit" of the show. Oh yes, I've got my fingers crossed for you.

Say, about Terri Moore being over here, well she was in Korea already, but she's not coming here. I guess she hasn't got the time for us. You wrote in your letter that you thought your letter didn't make too much sense, well don't worry about it, you first keep sending them, I really do enjoy them. Anyway, I'm a kind of guy who can understand letters that don't make sense, like I told you have my letters don't make sense either. So you see, we already have something in common.

Things here are just about the same as when I wrote last. Oh yes it is really raining tonight. It's a very good night to be home watching television, with their real good friend. Don't you agree with me? Remember how busy I told you I was. Well, the past three days I've even been busier yet.

You see we've got a General's inspection Wednesday and when a Marine has a Generals' inspection, He really has to look sharp. I sure am proud I am in this outfit instead of one of those other messed up branches of this service.

But then, with your sis being a Marine, you must hear that sort of stuff all the time. Well how are things that school these days? Are you one of those "brains" or are you liked my sister, just a normal student? Ha ha. Don't tell Thelma I said that she might get mad. Well that's about it for now, I'll write more next time. Take it easy and don't forget to answer soon.

Until next time,

Dave

P.S. DON'T FORGET A PICTURE OF YOURSELF

PSS I am enclosing a few pictures of myself. Not much, but it's the best I can do for now.

Terry Moore in *Peyton Place* (1957)

ENVELOPE 3

From:

PFC A. D. Katz 1368507

"A" Company, 3rd Tk BN

3RD Marine DIV. FMF

c/o FPO San Francisco, Calif.

Postmarked by US Navy, 24 May 1954

Addressed to Sheilah Bidnick

   1130 Forest Ave

   St. Louis (10) Mo.

May 23, 1954

Dear Sheilah,

Seems like every time I receive a letter from you it makes the day much brighter. Maybe it's because I really like to hear from you! You'll never know how much you're letters have changed me. I used to never care if we had mail call or not, but now, I get there an hour early to see if I got one from you.

Those pictures you sent of yourself were really nice, you not only write good letters, but your <u>cute</u>. The funniest part is I was surprised, just from the way you write I could tell that. Thanks for the pictures, and if you ever get any more you don't want I'll take them off your hands.

Speaking of pictures, if you send me one with your description I'll have it painted. These Japanese are really good at that. They are the closest thing too perfect I've seen yet Oh yes, don't worry about taking the place of Terri Moore. If you ask me, you could do that anytime. I'll be your favorite and anytime you want me. Haha.

I sure was glad to hear that your play was a real success. But after all with you in it what else could it have been but a hit. I'm sorry I couldn't have been there but the Marines just wouldn't let me. You understand don't you? I guess your Sister being a Marine is one of the reasons you understand my letters better than anyone else. Take for instance when I wrote you about the Generals' inspection. You knew all about what I was talking about, most people wouldn't even know what I meant.

Say Sheilah, what rank is your sister? I might have to SIR!

her for all I know. She is not an officer is she? That sure was quite a deal she got on that phone call to your mom. But then, the Marines always do things no others can do. Whoops, there I go bragging again. Seems like I'm always slipping that way.

Don't get mad when you read this next little bit but I'm sort of happy you weren't a brain. But just a very nice ordinary girl. Seems like I'm always having trouble getting along with the brainy people. Maybe it's because I'm not one myself. Any gal that can get "A"s in foods and gym, can do anything she supposes to do in future life. Don't you agree?

With you leaving the 19th of August, I sure hope I can get home before then. It would really make me feel bad if I couldn't meet you in person. But then, if you are gone when I get back to the states I'll hold off my leave until you get back. That's one way to get around missing the chance to meet you. See how much I think of you already? I'd set for California (Camp Pendleton) suffering to go home, just for you.

Well things here are just about the same. The only thing different is we're going out in the field more. I don't know why it is, but the time goes by so much quicker out there. Next Wednesday we're going out and staying for about a week, when we get back to our write and tell you all about what happened.

The weather has really been nice, just like summer. How is it at home? Has it warmed up yet? I don't know why it is, but I think summer is the best time of the year to be home. Maybe it's because a young man's fancy is nothing but having a good time, and last but not least making love to his girl. Do you think that's a good enough reason for wanting to come home? I have to drop a few lines to mom before lights go out so I'll close for now. Be a good girl, and stay happy.

Always Yours,

Dave

M48 Patton Tank, circa 1954

ENVELOPE 4

From:

PFC A. D. Katz 1368507

"A" Company, 3rd Tk BN

3RD Marine DIV. FMF

c/o FPO San Francisco, Calif.

Postmarked by US Navy, 13 July 1954

Addressed to   Sheilah Bidnick

1130 Forest Ave

St. Louis (10) Mo.

June 12, 1954

Hi Sheilah,

How is everything in Ole Saint Louis this fine summer day? I bet it's just right for picnics and outings isn't it? The best part I guess is school letting out. You like that don't you? You'll have nothing but spare time now. Things here are just fine. The only thing is they are really keeping us busy. I wrote you in my last letter that we were spending a lot of time in the <u>field</u>. Well what I mean is, we go out and live outdoors and all we do is train.

Yes even the tankers have to go. You see we take our tanks with us. The main reason we go out so much is because of all the new candidates just arrived, us "old salts" have to teach them all we know. All in all it is a lot of work and takes up just about all my spare time.

So if I don't answer your letters as promptly as I have been doing, you'll know the reason why.

To top it all off today we had an inspection by the Colonel, and as usual my platoon was the best. If it sounds like I'm bragging a little don't think me conceded, it's just that we always worked hard and the Marine Corp never gives out compliments, so we give out our own.

Say don't you worry about your pictures not looking good, I think they are wonderful, don't for get to send more so I can have one painted. Your mother was right these Japs really do a good job. I just can't wait to have one painted of you.

That sure sounded like a good deal Stix wanting you to try out for their fashion board. Did you make it? I really do hope so. I've had my fingers crossed hoping you did. Don't forget to let me know how everything turned out.

So your sister is just a PFC, well on her way, I'm glad. Because I sure don't like to salute women. I just don't feel right. That's more of the army trick. Of course don't tell her I said that, after she is a BAM and they are a little part of the Marine Corps.

That time has sure been going by fast. Why in just 18 more days I'll have been over here a little over a year. And unless something goes wrong, I ought to be home at least by August. That sure will be quite a day when I leave this place, it sure isn't anything like this State's. The only things that you've got you can do over here is drink and if you can drink enough, you sure get tired of that to.

Well I guess I asked for everything I got so I better quit complaining. Anyway I am sure you don't want to hear my troubles. Well that's about it for now, take it easy and be a good girl.

Until next time,
Dave

Letters from a Marine

ENVELOPE 5

From:

Cpl A. D. Katz 1368507

"A" Company, 3rd Tk BN

3RD Marine DIV. FMF

c/o FPO San Francisco, Calif.

Postmarked by US Navy, 12 July 1954

Addressed to Sheilah Bidnick

1130 Forest Ave

St. Louis (10) Mo.

July 8, 1954

Hello Sheilah,

While I've tried to write this letter for about a week now and this has been the first chance I've had really to sit down and write a halfway good letter. What I mean by a good letter is one over a page long. Maybe it's because the time are coming home is so close, but I just can't write anymore. Nothing new ever seems to happen. But I can tell from your pictures that you're a very <u>understanding</u> person and you'll realize my problem.

To begin with in just three more days we are going to Okinawa for training. And all we've been doing is been preparing for the trip. You see we are going to stay at least until July 30, which is Ok with me. Because when I get back I should have just a little less than a month to do over here. The latest word is August 28 but this time I'm not going to count on it until I'm aboard ship. One disappointment is enough for a while.

From how dark you look in your pictures you sure must have a real sunburn. I'm glad somebody has a chance to get out in the sun. Over here we haven't seen the sun in 25 days. All it ever does is rain. I want to explain that if sometimes I Sound bitter in my letters, it's nothing, it's just I've been here in Japan too long.
So you saw Toby out at the swimming pool. How's my little sister doing for herself? Did she have many boys with her? So is she still afraid of the water. Well, everyone has their own fears and I guess hers is water. We all can't be brave like Marines can we? Ha ha. (he was afraid of the water too; haha)

I hope you didn't tell your sister I called her a BAM. She might not like it. But then we are both Marines and she might not even not mind it. I don't know if I told you in my last letter, but I finally made <u>Corporal</u>. It does feel good to be finally giving orders instead of taking them, and we can't forget that extra $10 a month more on the pay. In my condition every little bit helps.

I'm sure sorry to hear that you will not have a senior book for when you graduate. But the main thing is being a senior anyway.

Well that's it for now. Take it easy and keep on enjoying yourself.

Until next time,
Dave

BAM – *A pejorative term for a Woman Marine, reportedly meaning broad assed Marine. Never used much in the presence of female Marines out of fear of bodily harm. Women Marine recruits in the 1960s, when it was most used, were taught that the letters meant "Beautiful American Marine". Known to have been used as early as World War II. It thankfully fell out of use in the late 20th Century**

ENVELOPE 6

From:

    Cpl A. D. Katz 1368507

    "A" Company, 3rd Tk BN

    3RD Marine DIV. FMF

    c/o FPO San Francisco, Calif.

Postmarked by US Navy, 31 July 1954

Addressed to Sheilah Bidnick

    1130 Forest Ave

    St. Louis (10) Mo.

July 29, 1954

Hello Sheilah,

It seems like every time I write you I'm always making excuses for not writing. But sometimes it's just impossible ever to get enough time to just write a few lines, especially when there's so little to write about.

You see it might sound selfish or something but all I can think about is coming home. Just the very thought of home makes me feel so good that I don't even like to talk about it for the year. I might go A.W.O.L. haha. No kidding I have really been making plans on all the things I want to do and every time when I think I'm done I add a few more things.

You wouldn't by any chance be interested in helping a Marine spend a few days on his long awaited leave with you? Don't think me forward or anything it's just that I want to know who my friends were before I come home. That's one thing a guy likes to know.

Sure was sorry to hear that you didn't get that job at Stix fashion board. In a way it's sort of my fault. I uncrossed my fingers too soon. I'm sorry it I'll try to do better next time.

I hope you won't be bored, but I'm going to write you a little about what happened on Okinawa. All in all it was a very nice trip, especially the weather. It didn't rain once and the temperature never dropped below 85°. To you that may not be hot but you see last month it rained 25 out of 30 days. As a matter of fact, it's raining right now. One thing I did get was a real nice suntan. For a little while I was so dark they couldn't tell me from a colored boy in the platoon.

I had to laugh at you're PS in your last letter. You asked me what I did on the 4th of July. To tell you the truth, nothing. All there is to do over here in Japan is drink, and that's one thing I never do is drink. Haha.

You might think I'm kidding you but I'm not. After all what would people say if they knew of Marine drank! So please don't tell anybody especially my sister. I don't think she'll understand, sisters never do. Don't you agree?

Say how did your little fishing trip turnout? Did you catch any fish or do you have a fish story to tell me? You know, about the big one that got away. Even if you didn't catch any I hope you had a good time. I know I always use to when I went fishing. We'd never catch anything but we'd sure have a good time.

What else is new at home? Anything exciting happening? If there is, don't for get to tell me about it. Well that's it for now, stay a <u>good</u> girl and be careful.

Yours As Always,
Dave

St Louis, MO in July, 1954

ENVELOPE 7

From:

Cpl A. D. Katz 1368507

"A" Company, 3rd TK BN

3RD Marine DIV. FMF

c/o FPO San Francisco, Calif.

Postmarked by US Navy, 24 August 1954

Addressed to Sheilah Bidnick

1130 Forest Ave

St. Louis (10) Mo.

AUG 24, 1954

Hi Sheilah,

I guess you are wondering why it takes so long for me to answer your letters. Well it's a long story and I hope you believe me. You see I've just about always got the same excuse. Because for the past two months we have gotten a whole bunch of "boot" replacements and they didn't know a thing. So we had to teach them all we know. And believe me it takes just about every bit of my time. Why I'm lucky I get time just to drop a few lines home once in a while.

Then to top it all off I've been catching quite a bit of guard duty. You see, it just doesn't pay to be such a good worker. They'll work you 24 hours a day if they had the chance. Now a little good news. The other day they set another date for leaving Japan. This time it will be sometime between the 5th and 11th of September. So if all goes well I ought to be home for the holidays. I think if they change and the date this time I'm going to <u>swim</u> home so help me!

After all it's already been 17 months since I've been home. After a guy stays away that long he kinda gets homesick once in a while. But then I really shouldn't be complaining. After all Marines are ever supposed to get homesick. You won't tell anybody I told you will you?
I guess by the time this letter gets to your home you'll be well on your way to Florida but it's better late than never. While we're on this subject of Florida, don't for get to tell me all about your trip. I'll bet you really had a good time at least I sure do hope so.

By the time you get back I ought to be ready to start my long trip home. So if you don't get a letter for a while, stand by, the <u>Marines</u> are about to land. I'd rather talk to you in person than right anyway. I never was a good letter writer. I hope I'm a better talker.

Well that about does it for now. I'll drop you a line just before I get ready to leave.

Yours Truly,
Dave

PS. That sure was quite a "fish story!"

1952-1954 Enlisted Basic Military Pay Chart

Monthly

Enlisted pay for less than 2 to over 6 years of service.

Pay Grade	Years of Service				
	Under 2	Over 2	Over 3	Over 4	Over 6
E-7	206.39	206.39	206.39	214.03	221.68
E-6	175.81	175.81	175.81	183.46	191.10
E-5	145.24	152.88	152.88	160.52	168.17
E-4	122.20	129.95	129.95	137.59	145.24
E-3	99.37	107.02	107.02	114.66	122.30
E-2 ➡	85.80	93.60	93.60	101.40	109.20
E-1	83.20	91.00	91.00	98.80	98.80

ENVELOPE 8

From:

    Cpl A. D. Katz 1368507

    Anti-Tank- Co, 3rd Marines (RIEF)

    3RD Marine DIV. FMF

    c/o FPO San Francisco, Calif.

Postmarked by US Navy, 2 September 1954

Addressed to Sheilah Bidnick

        1130 Forest Ave

        St. Louis (10) Mo.

PAGE 1 IS MISSING FROM THE ENVELOPE. The date is also unknown.

Page 2)… makes any sense. You sure must be a patient girl to put up with me for the past two months. After all you don't even know me, and here I am asking you to spend a few days of my leave with me. The only reason I'm explaining all this to you is that I don't want you to think I'm too forward. But then, I don't want you to think me backward either. It's just that all the girls I ever write or have ever gone out with think I'm a wolf so you can take your chances or just tell me not even to come visit you. I'm hoping you will because I'm a reformed man since I've been in the Marines. Why, I'm nearly a gentleman. Haha. While time is getting so short over here that I can barely count it on my fingers. From the last word it will be between the 15th and 20th. What really makes it hard is when it is so close that time goes by so slow. Each day seems like a week I guess I'm just too anxious. But then I've got a little right to be, it will be, by the time I get home, 18 long months since my last visit there. So you can see I'm not really as soft as it may sound.

I don't know what it is, but the weather has really been nice. Maybe it is a going away present from Japan.

For the first time in a long time me and a few of my buddies really had a good time on liberty. We went down to the ocean at Special Services Hotel and went swimming and ate and drank all day. The only thing missing was something I've nearly forgot what they look like, a real live American girl. But then you can't have everything all the time.

Well I said more than enough about myself in this letter let's now talk about a much better subject. You!

Don't forget to tell me everything you did and all that you saw on your whole trip. By the way have you graduated from school already or do you have a term or two left? If I'm not mistaken, my Sister Norma is going to graduate next term. She's really quite a brain. Do you know her? Well Sheilah, I can't think of much more to say other than that I'd like to be home for the holiday. Take it easy and keep on having a good time on your trip and at home.

As always,

Dave

CPSIA information can be obtained
at www.ICGtesting.com
Printed in the USA
LVHW040935221119
638065LV00005B/1896/P